MAXIMIZED MINUTES
MINUTES
FOR
BUSINESS

Edwin Louis Cole

MAXIMIZED MINUTES
FOR
BUSINESS

WHITAKER
HOUSE

MAXIMIZED MINUTES FOR BUSINESS

Christian Men's Network
P.O. Box 3
Grapevine, TX 76099
ChristianMensNetwork.com
facebook.com/edwinlouiscole/
facebook.com/ChristianMensNetwork/

ISBN: 978-1-64123-896-0
Printed in the United States of America
© 2022 by Edwin and Nancy Cole Legacy LLC

Whitaker House • 1030 Hunt Valley Circle • New Kensington, PA 15068
www.whitakerhouse.com

Library of Congress Control Number: 2022934869

1 2 3 4 5 6 7 8 9 10 11 ⨀ 29 28 27 26 25 24 23 22

CONTENTS

DREAMS:
THE SUBSTANCE OF EVERY
GREAT ACHIEVEMENT

A man's dreams of what he can accomplish in life are the basis for what he does accomplish in life.

And (Joseph) dreamed yet another dream, and told it his brethren, and said, Behold, I have dreamed a dream more; and, behold, the sun and the moon and the eleven stars made obeisance to me … And his brethren envied him; but his father observed the saying.

Genesis 37:9-11

DREAMS ARE THE SUBSTANCE OF EVERY GREAT ACHIEVEMENT.

Dreams are one of the major ways God speaks to men. Dreams can die, vanish, be taken away, but no man can live an exciting, fulfilled life without a dream.

Dreams realized are battles won. Real men dream the dream and do it.

And he said, Hear now my words: If there be a prophet among you, I the Lord will make myself known unto him in a vision, and will speak unto him in a dream.

Numbers 12:6

GOD-GIVEN DREAMS IN GOD-FAVORED MEN MAKE A GOD-BLESSED WORLD.

With God all things are possible. The Bible records that Israel "limited the holy one of Israel" (Psalm 78:41). In so doing, they limited themselves. If you limit yourself, you limit God. If you limit God, you limit yourself. Failure in faith limits man and God. You cannot limit God without limiting yourself.

Men find an unlimited life of peace, joy, and creativity through the study of God's Word. God knows no limitations, and a man following God doesn't either.

───────────────

But without faith it is impossible to please him: for he that cometh to God must believe that he is, and that he is a rewarder of them that diligently seek him.   Hebrews 11:6

All things are possible to him who believes.   Mark 9:23 NKJV

GOD PUTS NO LIMITS ON FAITH. FAITH PUTS NO LIMITS ON GOD.

Illusions of grandeur are not the same as visions of greatness. God-given dreams are the substance of great achievement, but God is not obligated to finish what he has not authored. God's Word is the substance of all faith and the basis for all behavior. A God-given dream will always be consistent with God's Word.

Jesus came as the truth and the life. Jesus never varies. Trust is extended to the limit of truth and no farther. God is truth and therefore totally trustworthy. Real men confirm their dreams through God's Word and commit to their dreams because of God's utter trustworthiness.

Jesus Christ the same yesterday, and today, and forever.   Hebrews 13:8

For I say ... to every man that is among you, not to think of himself more highly than he ought to think; but to think soberly.   Romans 12:3

WHATEVER GOD AUTHORS, HE WILL FINISH. WHAT GOD PROMISES, HE WILL FULFILL. WHATEVER IS COMMITTED TO HIM, HE WILL KEEP.

Dreams without goals are like engines without fuel. They go nowhere. Dreamers are divided by the "do's" and "cant's." Most dreamers who don't succeed are just lazy. W-o-r-k is not a four-letter obscenity.

Many men who work but don't see great accomplishments just didn't dream big enough. A dream becomes a work that becomes an achievement that is worthy of the dream.

Dreaming instead of doing is foolishness.   Ecclesiastes 5:7 TLB

Write the vision, and make it plain.
          Habakkuk 2:2

WHEN THE DREAM IS WRITTEN, IT BECOMES A GOAL. IF IT ISN'T IN WRITING, IT DOESN'T EXIST.

DEVELOPING A CHARACTER OF EXCELLENCE

God commits to character, not talent. Character undergirds talent, not vice versa. Your talent can take you where your character cannot sustain. Talent can bring fame. Fame can come for a moment, but greatness comes through longevity. That requires developing character.

You can develop talent when you are all alone, but you develop character when you are with others. You can tell the character of the man by the company he keeps. The Scripture says evil companionships will corrupt good manners.

A good name is rather to be chosen than great riches, and loving favour rather than silver and gold.   Proverbs 22:1

No accounting was required from the men who received the money to pay the workmen, because they acted with integrity.   2 Kings 12:15

CHARACTER IS MORE IMPORTANT THAN TALENT.

If character counts, then it counts for everything, and without it, nothing will count. Men of value are men with character. Their value is found in the truth upon which they build their lives. Only in Christ is real truth found, and from it comes a godly character built to last forever.

Whoever walks in integrity [with character] walks securely, but whoever takes crooked paths will be found out.

Proverbs 10:9 NIV

I urge you to live a life worthy of the calling you have received. Ephesians 4:1 NIV

WITHOUT GOOD CHARACTER, ALL MAN'S ACCOMPLISHMENTS ARE SHORT LIVED.

A man's integrity is shown by how he keeps his word more than in any other way. With his words, a man makes covenant. The handshake was originally a sign or signature of a covenant, not a mere greeting. Keeping covenant by keeping his word is the mark of a real man.

For by thy words thou shalt be justified, and by thy words thou shalt be condemned.   Matthew 12:37

Whoever keeps his mouth and his tongue keeps himself out of trouble.
                    Proverbs 21:23 ESV

A MAN'S WORD IS THE MEASURE OF HIS CHARACTER.

Truth is not an option in life — it is an absolute. Truth is not impersonal. Truth is personal.

Truth cannot be defeated. Truth will always be your vindication. There can be no foundation for a lasting and permanent life except truth.

A man's growth in the stature of his manhood is shown by the degree to which he builds his character and his word on truth.

I am the way, the truth, and the life: no man cometh unto the Father, but by me.
John 14:6

Jesus said, "If you hold to my teaching, you are really my disciples. Then you will know the truth, and the truth will set you free." John 8:31-32 NIV

TRUTH IS THE ONLY MORAL, ETHICAL, AND TRUE FOUNDATION TO A GOOD CHARACTER.

Our world has experienced a massive change of philosophy based on a change in morality. What the world cannot control, it will decriminalize and legalize. What the church cannot control, it will rationalize and psychologize. What men cannot control, they will demoralize and compromise.

Moral courage is needed to live in an immoral world. It may be tough to program your conscience to become aware of morality and immorality. It's tougher still to stand up to the immorality and keep yourself moral in spite of the pressures. Yet toughest of all is to live with the unmitigated consequences of immorality.

We live in tough times, but men of moral strength can still thrive. You are God's moral agent. Let your light shine.

I want the company of the godly men and women in the land; they are the true nobility.   Psalm 16:3 TLB

I will make the godly of the land my heroes and invite them to my home.
                                   Psalm 101:6 TLB

THE DARKER THE NIGHT, THE BRIGHTER THE LIGHT.

Most men could have done more but settled for less.

Patience in a test most often determines the difference between good and best. Our best is when we can do no better. God's best is more than good—it is righteous.

[You] have need of patience that after [you] have done the will of God [you] might receive the promise.

Hebrews 10:36

To win the contest you must deny yourselves many things that would keep you from doing your best.

1 Corinthians 9:25 TLB

GOOD IS OFTEN THE ENEMY OF BEST.

God commits to faithfulness, not talent. God teaches us that if we are not faithful in that which is another man's, we will not qualify for that which is our own. True in business as well as in life.

God promises that when we prove faithful in the little things, he can reward us with the greater. With greater things comes greater responsibility, and requires a greater level of faithfulness, and a greater measure of character.

He who is faithful in what is least is faithful also in much; and he who is unjust in what is least is unjust also in much. Therefore if you have not been faithful in the unrighteous mammon, who will commit to your trust the true riches? And if you have not been faithful in what is another man's, who will give you what is your own?   Luke 16:10-12 NKJV

And the things that you have heard from me among many witnesses, commit these to faithful men who will be able to teach others also.   2 Timothy 2:2 NKJV

FAITHFULNESS IS THE CORNERSTONE OF CHARACTER.

DEALING WITH SELF

Honoring God in private is shown by a man's decisions in public. Is what a man does in private his own business? No, not true. No man lives or dies to himself. What he does in private affects him, affects his decisions, and affects society when it becomes public. Whatever is done in secret will one day be shouted from the housetops. In politics, what a man practices in private is how he will vote in public. That affects nations.

A man who honors God privately will show it by making good decisions publicly.

A good man out of the good treasure of the heart bringeth forth good things: and an evil man out of the evil treasure bringeth forth evil things.   Matthew 12:35

What you have said in the dark will be heard in the daylight, and what you have whispered in the ear in the inner rooms will be proclaimed from the roofs.
                                    Luke 12:3 NIV

PRIVATE PHILOSOPHY DETERMINES PUBLIC PERFORMANCE.

What you believe has the power to attract or repel. If you believe God is capricious and condemnatory, it will repel you from belief in him. But if you believe that he is a loving and forgiving Father, Savior, and Lord, your attraction to him will know no bounds.

Some men gamble, convinced they'll "hit the big one," then wonder why their wives leave, work is a struggle, and their kids don't respect them. Their wrong beliefs are working against them. Studying and believing God's Word is the least expensive thing a man will ever do. Unbelief is the most expensive commodity in life.

For as he (a man) thinketh in his heart, so is he.   Proverbs 23:7

Since, then, you have been raised with Christ, set your hearts on things above, where Christ is, seated at the right hand of God. Set your minds on things above, not on earthly things. Put to death, therefore, whatever belongs to your earthly nature: sexual immorality, impurity, lust, evil desires and greed, which is idolatry.

Colossians 3:1-2, 5 NIV

ALL WRONG CONDUCT IS BASED ON WRONG BELIEVING.

The Bible is the one book that can tell you who you really are. You'll go much farther in life if what you think about yourself is based on what God thinks about you.

Some of the strongest words you can confess are: "I am who God says I am, I have what God says I have, and I can do what God says I can do, because God's grace is sufficient in my life."

For now we see only a reflection as in a mirror; then we shall see face to face. Now I know in part; then I shall know fully, even as I am fully known.
1 Corinthians 13:12 NIV

I can do all things through him who gives me strength.   Philippians 4:13 NIV

ONLY THREE OPINIONS IN LIFE MATTER — WHAT YOU THINK ABOUT GOD, WHAT GOD THINKS ABOUT YOU, WHAT YOU THINK ABOUT YOURSELF.

Words have creative power. That's why life and death are in the power of the tongue.

Two simple words, "Thank you," have the ability to create good will, exemplify courtesy, and produce intimate relationships. Taking not much more than a blink of an eye, those two little words said in earnest can tear down ill feelings, destroy bad attitudes, and bring goodness in life.

One of them, when he saw he was healed, came back, praising God in a loud voice. He threw himself at Jesus' feet and thanked him.   Luke 17:15-16 NIV

The tongue has the power of life and death, and those who love it will eat its fruit.   Proverbs 18:21 NIV

Giving thanks always and for everything to God the Father in the name of our Lord Jesus Christ.   Ephesians 5:20 ESV

GRATITUDE CONFIRMS RELATIONSHIPS.

Your yoke is what you believe, and what you believe determines the burdens you carry in life. You pay the highest price for the lowest way of living. Sin shows only its pleasures but never its consequences. After the pleasure of sin is gone, the consequences can live on for a lifetime or an eternity.

Take my yoke upon you and learn from me, for I am gentle and humble in heart, and you will find rest for your souls. For my yoke is easy and my burden is light.

Matthew 11:29-30 NIV

THE YOKE YOU WEAR DETERMINES THE BURDEN YOU BEAR.

Parents don't have to teach children to disobey because all humanity is negative by nature. We must be converted from the negative to the positive. Children know this. They never ask parents for something only once. They ask until the parent is converted. Salesmen learn how to convert customers from a negative to a positive.

Because we are negative by nature, it is often easier to believe a lie than the truth. We often believe we are escaping *from* something, when God sees it as going *to* something. Ask God to convert your negatives to positives. Conversion is necessary to human life.

And he said, "What comes out of a person is what defiles him. For from within, out of the heart of man, come evil thoughts, sexual immorality, theft, murder, adultery, coveting, wickedness, deceit, sensuality, envy, slander, pride, foolishness. All these evil things come from within, and they defile a person." Mark 7:20-23 ESV

Jesus said to him, "I am the way, and the truth, and the life. No one comes to the Father except through me." John 14:6 ESV

WE ARE NEGATIVE BY NATURE BECAUSE WE ARE CONDITIONED TO FAILURE AND SUBJECT TO SIN.

God loves us whether we meet his conditions or not. If we do not meet his conditions through faith, we cannot obtain his promises. Whether we are rich or poor, have or have not, has nothing to do with God's love, but with the condition of our faith. God's love and his salvation is lavishly bestowed on us with unmerited favor. Just as children must meet parental conditions, men must meet God's conditions to receive his blessings.

Receiving God's promises requires conditions. Our salvation is not based on our goodness, but on his gracious, unconditional love.

We know and rely on the love God has for us. God is love. Whoever lives in love lives in God, and God in them.

1 John 4:16 NIV

Whatever we ask we receive from him, because we keep his commandments and do what pleases him.   1 John 3:22 ESV

GOD'S LOVE IS UNCONDITIONAL. HIS PROMISES ARE CONDITIONAL.

OBEDIENT ACTION

We only have the now because the past is irretrievable, and there is no tomorrow; for when tomorrow comes, it is "today."

We learn from the past to do in the present what will provide for the future. What we do today is the most important thing.

But encourage one another daily, as long as it is called "Today," so that none of you may be hardened by sin's deceitfulness.
                                    Hebrews 3:13 NIV

Behold, now is the accepted time, behold, now is the day of salvation.
                                    2 Corinthians 6:2

Therefore do not worry about tomorrow, for tomorrow will worry about itself. Each day has enough trouble of its own.
                                    Matthew 6:34 NIV

TODAY IS THE ONLY DAY THERE IS, AND THERE IS NO SECOND CHANCE TO LIVE TODAY.

When Jesus said we obey him if we love him, he was saying that obedience is the evidence of love. Some men won't give financially to the work of the Lord, and instead try to sacrifice by prayer what they lose through disobedience. Then they wonder why God doesn't answer their prayers.

A ton of prayer will never produce what an ounce of obedience will. God's manifesting himself in your business is based on obedience. "You reap what you sow" is a Kingdom principle. Acting on Kingdom principles leads to success.

If you love me, obey my commandments.
John 14:15 NLT

Does the LORD delight in burnt offerings and sacrifices as much as in obeying the LORD? To obey is better than sacrifice. 1 Samuel 15:22 NIV

Do not be deceived: God is not mocked, for whatever one sows, that will he also reap. Galatians 6:7 ESV

YOU CANNOT COMPENSATE BY SACRIFICE WHAT YOU LOSE THROUGH DISOBEDIENCE.

Jesus gave the Church one prayer request: to pray for laborers. The harvest is ripe. It's there. What we need is to be prepared with laborers.

Similarly, opportunities are not the problem in business. Opportunities happen. Readiness and labor are the issue. Men too often miss opportunities because they are not prepared. Tomorrow's opportunities await. But when tomorrow becomes today, men are too busy with yesterday.

Men also miss opportunities because they come in the form of labor. Opportunities are an invitation to work. No opportunity is seized without it. Pray you'll be prepared, then work to seize the opportunity when it comes.

The harvest truly is great, but the labourers are few: pray ye therefore the Lord of the harvest, that he would send forth labourers into his harvest.   Luke 10:2

DON'T PRAY FOR OPPORTUNITIES. PRAY YOU'LL BE READY WHEN OPPORTUNITIES COME.

Too many men look for God to lead them through some spectacular means, but the greatest work the Holy Spirit does is to make men "Christlike." To hear the Holy Spirit requires being immersed in God's Word.

The Holy Spirit will never lead you to do anything contrary to the Word of God, inconsistent with the will of God, or opposed to the ways of God.

The greatest way to hear from God is to be consistently led by the "still small voice" of the Holy Spirit that is confirmed in God's Word.

And after the earthquake a fire; but the Lord was not in the fire: and after the fire a still small voice.   1 Kings 19:12

IF YOU LOOK FOR THE SUPERNATURAL ONLY IN THE SPECTACULAR, YOU'LL MISS THE HOLY SPIRIT.

Though timeless in himself, God shows great respect for time in dealing with men. Time, like fruit, ripens. Fruit spoils if picked too late or is sour if picked too early. To be the right man in the right place at the wrong time can lead to failure. Just like saying the right thing at the wrong time can be called nagging.

God's appointed time for men to enjoy the blessings of his grace is to live in the now, led by his Spirit, captured by his all-sufficient grace.

For the vision is yet for an appointed time.   Habakkuk 2:3

Be ready in season and out of season.
                              2 Timothy 4:2 NKJV

TIMING IS THE ESSENTIAL INGREDIENT IN SUCCESS: BEING THE RIGHT MAN, AT THE RIGHT TIME, IN THE RIGHT PLACE.

Heroism is personified in military cemetery crosses marking men who laid down their lives for people they did not know. First responders daily risk their lives for people they have never met.

The one act greater than all is a wonder no man can comprehend. God came to earth in the form of a man and laid down his life on Calvary's cross to prove his love for you.

To him that overcometh will I grant to sit with me in my throne, even as I also overcame, and am set down with my Father in his throne.　　　　　　Revelations 3:21

Greater love hath no man than this, that a man lay down his life for his friends.
　　　　　　　　　　　　　　John 15:13

I pray that you, being rooted and established in love, may have power, together with all the Lord's holy people, to grasp how wide and long and high and deep is the love of Christ, and to know this love that surpasses knowledge.　　　　　　Ephesians 3:17-19 NIV

HEROES ARE MEN WHO ACT IN A MOMENT OF TIME ON A NEED GREATER THAN SELF.

A tightrope walker crossed a waterfall on a wire stretched across it. He made it across and back, then picked up a chair and asked how many thought he could make it again. The crowd that had gathered applauded. He set down the chair and picked up the handles of a wheelbarrow and asked again. They cheered. Then he asked, "Who will be the first to get in?"

The only Scripture you really believe is the one you obey. Hearing from God through his Word, then acting in faith may seem gutsy, but it's the surest road to success.

Someone will say, "You have faith, and I have works." Show me your faith without your works, and I will show you my faith by my works ... But do you want to know, O foolish man, that faith without works is dead? Was not Abraham our father justified by work?... And the Scripture was fulfilled which says, "Abraham believed God, and it was accounted to him for righteousness." ... You see then that a man is justified by works, and not by faith only.   James 2:18-24 NKJV

BELIEF IS NOT FAITH UNTIL IT IS ACTED UPON.

People who wait for perfect conditions never get anything done. You don't wait until you have enough money to get married or have kids or start a business, or else you'll never do it. You just get married and have kids and start your business. Imperfection is the natural state of man. Act in obedience to God's Spirit and his Word and allow God's grace to compensate for all the blemishes, faults, defects, and pain.

He that observeth the wind shall not sow; and he that regardeth the clouds shall not reap.   Ecclesiastes 11:4

If you wait for perfect conditions, you will never get anything done.
                    Ecclesiastes 11:4 TLB

IF YOU WAIT FOR PERFECT CONDITIONS, YOU'LL NEVER GET ANYTHING DONE.

CRISIS AND CHANGE

It is the nature of God to changes things in our lives for the good. All trials and temptations will end positively if committed to God. God always starts on the positive and ends on the positive.

There is pressure in change, but change is the only constant in maturity. People who refuse to change cannot grow physically, mentally, emotionally, morally, or maritally.

Without growth there is no maturing.

But we all, with unveiled face, beholding as in a mirror the glory of the Lord, are being transformed into the same image from glory to glory, just as by the Spirit of the Lord.　2 Corinthians 3:18 NKJV

Until we all attain… to a mature man, to the measure of the stature which belongs to the fullness of Christ… no longer to be children… we are to grow up in all aspects into Him who is the head, even Christ.
Ephesians 4:13-15 NASB

CHANGE IS THE ONLY CONSTANT IN MATURITY.

Men can think about change, pray about change, promise to change, imagine what change is like, decide to change, but it is never change until it is change.

Too many men give themselves credit for their intentions but not for their actions. They judge others for their actions, but themselves for their intentions.

Let us not love in word, neither in tongue; but in deed and in truth.   1 John 3:18

Very truly I tell you, whoever believes in me will do the works I have been doing, and they will do even greater things than these, because I am going to the Father.
                              John 14:12 NIV

CHANGE IS NOT CHANGE UNTIL IT IS CHANGE.

Crisis is normal to life. The crisis of change is the only process by which we go from transient to permanent, from misunderstanding to understanding.

Each step in growth comes via crisis. Birth to infancy, infancy to childhood, childhood to adolescence. Each change undertaken has its own measure of change and crisis. Likewise, each plateau in business brings the need for new equipment, personnel, techniques, products.

Successful people recognize crisis as a time for change — from lesser to greater, smaller to bigger. Rather than fight or flight, successful men use it as a time for growth.

In the world [you] shall have tribulation: but be of good cheer; I have overcome the world.   John 16:33

CRISIS IS NORMAL TO LIFE. ALL CHANGE COMES BY WAY OF CRISIS.

The difference between the ideal and the real is where life's disappointments are found. You have to reconcile the discrepancy between them.

People tend to create the ideal — then live the real. New employees who discover flaws or faults without reconciling it in their minds will allow the disappointment to degenerate into resistance to authority or rebellion against it.

Reconciliation is the ministry of the Lord Jesus Christ and is one of the reasons men cannot live without him.

———————————

God was reconciling the world to himself in Christ, not counting people's sins against them. And he has committed to us the message of reconciliation.

2 Corinthians 5:19 NIV

DISAPPOINTMENTS IN LIFE ARE NOT BASED ON WHAT YOU FIND BUT ON WHAT YOU EXPECT TO FIND.

In the heat of the pressure, problems loom larger, crises seem more severe. When time is condensed, compacted, everything said and done is magnified out of all proportion. The further from the situation, in time or distance, the smaller it appears.

Men who become heroes and champions, who achieve great things, are those who learned how to handle pressure.

The difference in sports between winners and losers, and in business between those who succeed and fail, is often found in their ability to handle pressure.

And being in an agony he prayed more earnestly: and his sweat was as it were great drops of blood falling down to the ground.   Luke 22:44

If you faint in the day of adversity, Your strength is small.   Proverbs 24:10 NKJV

PRESSURE ALWAYS MAGNIFIES.

Success is not based on the ability to say yes, but on the ability to say no. Resisting the extraneous, illegitimate, and unnecessary, allows for occupation with the productive, positive, and vital.

The strength of glue can be tested by gluing two items together then trying to pull them apart. The strength of business partners is shown when they resist the pressures that try to pull them apart. The strength of the employee or CEO is shown by their resistance to traits and attitudes that try to pollute or destroy them. Character resists bad company.

Therefore submit to God. Resist the devil and he will flee from you.   James 4:7 NKJV

My son, if sinners entice you, Do not consent.   Proverbs 1:10

Finally, my brethren, be strong in the Lord and in the power of His might. Put on the whole armor of God, that you may be able to stand against the wiles of the devil.
                                         Ephesians 6:10-11 NKJV

O man of God, flee these things and pursue righteousness, godliness, faith, love, patience, gentleness.   1 Timothy 6:11 NKJV

ALL TESTING IS BASED ON RESISTANCE.

Worry centers on self. Prayer centers on God. Anxiety is self-centered. Faith is God-centered.

Worry is a substitute for prayer. Prayerlessness in its most common form is a form of hiding. Prayer depends on relationship — God with man, man with God. Wishing is not the same as praying. Prayer is not something to engage in only when it is convenient. God must be sought after to be found.

Men who depend on money instead of God are unwilling to recognize the Lord as the source of true wealth. A wise man makes God his first resource. God must be the source of all, or else he is the solution to nothing.

Don't worry about anything; instead, pray about everything. Tell God what you need, and thank him for all he has done.

Philippians 4:6 NLT

Rejoice always, pray without ceasing, give thanks in all circumstances for this is the will of God in Christ Jesus concerning you.

1 Thessalonians 5:16-18 NKJV

WORRY IS A SUBSTITUTE FOR PRAYER.

Joseph rose to become second in command in all of Egypt, but only after he faced jealousy, anger, envy, slander, betrayal, rejection, humiliation, cruelty, injustice, imprisonment, conspiracies, enslavement, entrapment, fraud, false accusations, false friends, malice, and petty, lustful spirits. Joseph persevered. His faith never ended.

You're never too young, too old, too poor, or too rich for God to make your dream a reality. God does not play favorites. Remember, what God authors, he will finish. What God promises, he will fulfill. What is committed to him, God will keep.

Blessed is the one who perseveres under trial.   James 1:12 NIV

But he who endures to the end shall be saved.   Matthew 24:13 NKJV

God does not show favoritism.
                    Romans 2:11 NIV

Commit your work to the LORD, and your plans will be established.
                    Proverbs 16:3 ESV

PERSEVERANCE WILL ALWAYS OUTLAST PERSECUTION.

WISDOM

The internal is more important than the external. The unseen is more important than the seen. And the spirit is more important than the body.

The intangibles of life are more important because they're what make the tangibles possible. Wisdom is more valuable than rubies; love is superior to sex; respect is more substantial than money; a good name is more to be chosen than riches; honor is more valuable than position.

Wisdom is one of the intangibles, but Scripture calls wisdom the "principal thing."

So we fix our eyes not on what is seen, but on what is unseen, since what is seen is temporary, but what is unseen is eternal.
2 Corinthians 4:18 NIV

Wisdom is more precious than rubies, and nothing you desire can compare with her.   Proverbs 8:11 NIV

Wisdom is the principal thing; Therefore get wisdom. And in all your getting, get understanding.   Proverbs 4:7 NKJV

THINGS VISIBLE ARE
CREATED FROM WHAT
IS INVISIBLE—
SO THE INTANGIBLES
ARE ALWAYS MORE
IMPORTANT THAN THE
TANGIBLES.

Wisdom, not money, is man's basic need. You can have money, but to use it without wisdom is to be in constant need without financial security. Lack of wisdom has killed more than one business.

In addition to wisdom, men need understanding. Wisdom is the right use of knowledge, and understanding is applied, anointed common sense. Wisdom was with God in creating our world. God spoke the Word in creation. The one true source of wisdom is God's Word.

Happy is the man who finds wisdom, And the man who gains understanding… Length of days is in her right hand, In her left hand riches and honor. Her ways are ways of pleasantness, And all her paths are peace.   Proverbs 3:13, 16-17 NKJV

By wisdom the LORD laid the earth's foundations, by understanding he set the heavens in place.   Proverbs 3:19 NIV

WISDOM GIVES A LONG, GOOD LIFE, RICHES, HONOR, PLEASURE, AND PEACE.

Error and vice are contagious. Righteousness and knowledge are not. Associations can be infectious. When asked, wise men are willing to impart their wisdom for the benefit of others. Fools pollute people. People pollution is the worst kind of contamination.

Do not be misled: "Bad company corrupts good character."
1 Corinthians 15:33 NIV

He that walketh with wise men shall be wise; but a companion of fools will be destroyed. Proverbs 13:20

BE WITH WISE MEN
AND BECOME WISER.
BE WITH A FOOL AND
BECOME FOOLISH.

Assumption is based on internal subjective opinion. Knowledge comes from external objective fact. Knowledge is discovered by seeking, by studying, and through applying yourself to learn.

Skill is the ability to put knowledge into action. Practice is the highest level of learning and is the lifestyle of leaders. Acting on assumption is like building a second story on a vacant lot.

Therefore my people are gone into captivity, because they have no knowledge: and their honourable men are famished; and their multitude dried up with thirst.
Isaiah 5:13

The fear of the LORD is the beginning of knowledge, but fools despise wisdom and instruction. Proverbs 1:7

Because they hated knowledge and did not choose the fear of the Lord…they shall eat the fruit of their way…; but whoever listens to me will dwell secure and will be at ease, without dread of disaster.
Proverbs 1:29, 33 ESV

ASSUMPTION IS LIFE'S LOWEST LEVEL OF KNOWLEDGE.

Humans are negative by nature. Often, what we don't understand, we are against. True in your family. True in your business.

Good employees are informed employees. To get good cooperation, people need good understanding. Thoroughly explain when you'll launch the new product, set new plans, and make clear why policies are set. Happy campers are the best kind.

And this is the condemnation, that light is come into the world, and men loved darkness rather than light.   John 3:19

My people are destroyed from lack of knowledge.   Hosea 4:6 NIV

BECAUSE PEOPLE ARE
NEGATIVE BY NATURE,
WHAT WE DON'T
UNDERSTAND WE ARE
AGAINST.

When men lack wisdom, they make errors in strategy. God always gives a strategy for victory. God's wisdom is the strategy. His glory is in the victory. Moses, Gideon, David, Elijah—all achieved great victories in their lives because God gave them the strategy necessary to obtain it.

God is generous. God lavishes his grace on sinners. He gives great glory to his saints. You don't have to convince God to give you what he has already said is his good pleasure to give. Men pray for wisdom. God gives wisdom for a strategy that leads to victory.

If any of you lacks wisdom, let him ask of God, who gives to all liberally and without reproach, and it will be given to him.
Mark James 1:5 NKJV

It is your Father's good pleasure to give you the kingdom. Luke 12:32 NKJV

MEN PRAY FOR VICTORY. GOD GIVES A STRATEGY.

RIGHT DECISIONS

The power of choice is our only true freedom in life. Choices determine conduct, character, and destiny. Choices are based on what you believe. What you believe about God, yourself, and others has the greatest potential for good or harm in your life.

Choices have consequences. It is your responsibility alone to change your choices to change your future. You can complain about constraints within which you're forced to live with, but regardless of your circumstances, you still have choices.

Refusing to exercise your power of choice allows others to exercise it for you and allows them to create your world. When you allow others to create your world for you, they will always make it too small.

Choose for yourselves this day whom you will serve.   Joshua 24:15 NIV

Elijah went before the people and said, "How long will you waver between two opinions? If the LORD is God, follow him; but if Baal is God, follow him."
                              1 Kings 18:21 NIV

CHOICES DETERMINE OUR DESTINY.

Free will separates humans from animals. God brought us into the world so we could choose him. Once we make the choice, we become the servant to that choice and our life changes for the good. Avoiding a decision is a decision in itself. Covering up, lying, or escaping, the choice will still make you the servant of that choice. You're simply working harder to cover up, lie, or escape.

Choose responsibility, make right decisions, and you'll be the servant of those choices and become a trustworthy man. It's all within our power. Our choice. You decide.

———————————

All things are lawful for me, but all things are not helpful. All things are lawful for me, but I will not be brought under the power of any.   1 Corinthians 6:12 NKJV

EVERYTHING IN LIFE IS UNDER OUR POWER OF CHOICE, BUT ONCE WE MAKE THE CHOICE, WE BECOME SERVANTS TO THAT CHOICE.

Whatever your life is today is the sum total of all the choices either you have made, others have made for you, or the words you have spoken or that have been spoken to you that you received into your life. To change a life, change the choices. For those to change, attitude must change. To grow in life, attitude determines altitude.

People who refuse to change can't grow — physically, mentally, emotionally, morally, maritally. Without growth there is no maturing and little success.

A fool despises his father's instruction, but whoever heeds reproof is prudent.
                                        Proverbs 15:5

Jesus said, "And no one puts new wine into old wineskins. If he does, the wine will burst the skins—and the wine is destroyed, and so are the skins. But new wine is for fresh wineskins."   Mark 2:22 ESV

A good man's mind is filled with honest thoughts; an evil man's mind is crammed with lies.   Proverbs 12:5 TLB

WHERE YOU ARE TODAY IS THE RESULT OF YOUR CHOICES YESTERDAY.

Change your choices, change your words, change your life. Every word has creative power. Scripture says the tongue has the power of life and death.

Once you make the choice to build a new life, change your words. Our words build our lives. Every word we speak releases creative power and sets the world around us in motion. To change our life, we must change the choices we make and the words we use.

From the fruit of his lips a man enjoys good things, but the desire of the faithless is violence. Proverbs 13:2

For by your words you will be acquitted, and by your words you will be condemned. Matthew 12:37 NIV

Who being the brightness of his glory, and the express image of his person, and upholding all things by the word of his power. Hebrews 1:3

LIFE IS COMPOSED OF OUR CHOICES AND CONSTRUCTED BY OUR WORDS.

Communication: When communication stops, abnormality sets in. Exchange: In salvation, Jesus exchanged his life for ours. In biology, we exchange oxygen for carbon dioxide. In business, every sale is an exchange, and every step of growth is made by way of exchanging the old for the new. Balance: Balanced diet, balanced spirit, balanced life. Agreement: The place of agreement is the place of power. Disagreement produces powerlessness.

Employees in agreement with employers can produce great profits, but disunity, confusion, misunderstanding, and imbalance brings loss of the ability to produce.

Reliable communication permits progress. Proverbs 13:17 TLB

God made him who had no sin to be sin for us, so that in him we might become the righteousness of God.
2 Corinthians 5:21 NIV

If two of you on earth agree about anything they ask for, it will be done for them by my Father in heaven. Matthew 18:19 NIV

COMMUNICATION IS THE BASIS OF LIFE.

EXCHANGE IS THE PROCESS OF LIFE.

BALANCE IS THE KEY TO LIFE.

AGREEMENT IS THE POWER OF LIFE.

LEADERSHIP

Proving precedes promotion. Proving comes through testing. To promote what is not proven is to promote the untested. If you promote what has not been tested, you will be tested on what you promote.

Men prove God by taking him at his Word. God proves men by their obedience to his Word.

———

Confidence in an unfaithful man in time of trouble is like a broken tooth, and a foot out of joint.   Proverbs 25:19

We are not trying to please people but God, who tests our hearts.
                    1 Thessalonians 2:4 NIV

I the LORD search the heart and examine the mind, to reward each person according to their conduct, according to what their deeds deserve.   Jeremiah 17:10 NIV

PROMOTE ONLY WHAT IS PROVEN.

Mediocre men want authority without accountability. To give authority without accountability is like giving a match to an arsonist. It invites anarchy.

Authority can only be given to those who accept responsibility, and accountability is a requirement of responsibility. Likewise, you cannot hold someone accountable for something for which they were not responsible. Responsibility without accountability is equally an error. A faithful man is an accountable man, and his faithfulness is the cornerstone of good character.

Never give authority without accountability. God doesn't—don't you.

For unto whomsoever much is given, of him shall be much required. Luke 12:48

GOD NEVER GIVES AUTHORITY WITHOUT ACCOUNTABILITY.

The man who knows how will always have a job; the man who knows why will always be his boss. You can learn how to do something, but if you master the pattern by which it works, or the principle on which it rests, you will always rise above your peers. Open yourself to new ideas. Learn to adapt to new technologies. Realize there may be more to what you think you know.

Stubbornness is the core of ignorance because an ignorant person is too stubborn to learn. Shun ignorance! Read. Learn the principles. Master the patterns. Have the courage to change.

To answer before listening—that is folly and shame.　　　　Proverbs 18:13 NIV

Do your best to present yourself to God as one approved, a worker who does not need to be ashamed and who correctly handles the word of truth.　　　2 Timothy 2:15 NIV

And the Lord said, Who then is that faithful and wise steward, whom his lord shall make ruler over his household, to give them their portion of meat in due season?　　Luke 12:42

IT IS HARD TO TELL SOMEONE SOMETHING THEY THINK THEY ALREADY KNOW.

Availability is not the greatest need in business, teachability is. A person may be available, but if he cannot be taught or is not willing to learn, it's no wonder he is available. No one wants someone who prefers to be ignorant. The man you want to be, and the man you want working for you, is the man who studies to "show himself approved."

———————————

To learn, you must want to be taught.
Proverbs 12:1 TLB

My son, if you accept my words and store up my commands within you, turning your ear to wisdom and applying your heart to understanding—indeed, if you call out for insight and cry aloud for understanding, and if you look for it as for silver and search for it as for hidden treasure, then you will understand the fear of the Lord and find the knowledge of God.   Proverbs 2:1-5 NIV

TO LEARN YOU MUST WANT TO BE TAUGHT.

In the parable of the pounds and talents, two of the three men invested and received a hundred percent increase. They each spoke just fifteen words, because their work proved their performance. The third man used forty-four words to give an excuse for his lack of productivity.

Jesus said the servant who did nothing was wicked and slothful, insolent and indolent. There are reasons successful men are productive. Others have only excuses.

A man entrusted his wealth to his servants. Two servants who made investments said, "See, I have gained more." The man who did not invest said, "Master, I knew that you are a hard man, harvesting where you have not sown and gathering where you have not scattered seed. So I was afraid and went out and hid your gold in the ground…."

Matthew 25:14-29 *condensed from* NIV

THE MAN WHO TALKS THE MOST USUALLY DOES THE LEAST.

The character of the leader is shown in the characteristics of his family and his work. Where change is necessary, it must come voluntarily from the top, or it will come involuntarily from the bottom. Revelation is always better than revolution.

———

When the righteous are in authority, the people rejoice: but when the wicked beareth rule, the people mourn.

Proverbs 29:2

THE CHARACTERISTICS OF THE KINGDOM EMANATE FROM THE CHARACTER OF THE KING.

Write the vision you have for your future, confess it and commit it to paper, and it will become achievable. If you don't say it, you won't feel responsible or compelled to do it.

Confess the positive promises of God's Word, believing them to materialize in your own life, and you will commit yourself to them.

For the Lord God is a sun and shield; the Lord bestows favor and honor; no good thing does he withhold from those whose walk is blameless.   Psalm 84:11 NIV

Thou art snared with the words of thy mouth, thou art taken with the words of thy mouth.   Proverbs 6:2

The LORD said to me, "You have seen correctly, for I am watching to see that my word is fulfilled."   Jeremiah 1:12 NIV

YOU ARE COMMITTED TO WHAT YOU CONFESS.

You can have the finest management program, an excellent policy and procedures manual, the best organizational structure and most well-thought-out marketing plan, but with poor personnel, it will wallow in mediocrity or fail.

Finding and training people is a lifelong duty if you intend to be successful. The basic pattern for management is — win them, train them, send them. It's the same in sports, customer service, restaurants, and it's the same for parents.

Train people, give them responsibility, and have them account for it.

Do you see a man who excels in his work? He will stand before kings; He will not stand before unknown men.

Proverbs 22:29 NKJV

Can two walk together, unless they are agreed? Amos 3:3 NKJV

PERSONNEL IS ALWAYS THE PROBLEM, AND PERSONNEL IS ALWAYS THE SOLUTION.

God always works according to a pattern and based on a principle of his kingdom. Learn his patterns and principles, and your life becomes productive, maximized, and successful. But live by personality, theory, and circumstance, and your life is confusing and driven by every wind of change. The more we base our lives on principles and less upon personalities, the straighter our course will be.

If we only learn to respond to specific circumstances, we will never know enough to cover every situation. But with God's patterns and principles, we are equipped to handle every situation and issue.

All the principles and promises of the Bible are the keys to the kingdom. Finding God's pattern for your life and basing your faith on his principles brings success.

For He said, "See that you make all things according to the pattern shown you on the mountain."

Hebrews 8:5 NKJV

May God's mercy and peace be upon all of you who live by this principle.

Galatians 6:16 TLB

EVERYTHING GOD DOES, HE DOES ACCORDING TO A PATTERN AND BASED ON A PRINCIPLE OF HIS KINGDOM.

SETBACKS AND FAILURES

Do not despise failure. Accept failures and use them as a catalyst to success. Do not fear failure. Fear of failure is a sure way to live with failure. Do not live with failure. Bury failures and keep on going. Jesus said, "Let the dead bury the dead." That means, don't live with death, not even the death of a dream or an idea. Leave it, and move on to find success after success.

Successful men know that each failure brings them closer to success. Better to try to do something and fail, than quit and succeed in doing nothing. Success is born out of failure.

Jesus said to him, "Let the dead bury their own dead, but you go and proclaim the kingdom of God." Luke 9:60 NIV

Though he may stumble, he will not fall, for the Lord upholds him with his hand.
Psalm 37:24 NIV

FAILURE IS THE WOMB
OF SUCCESS.

You don't drown by falling in the water. You drown by staying there.

Don't quit on God. He doesn't quit on you. Quitting on God is quitting on yourself, and quitting on yourself is quitting on God. God never quits, and neither should you.

Even when we are too weak to have any faith left, he remains faithful to us and will help us, for he cannot disown us who are part of himself, and he will always carry out his promises to us.

2 Timothy 2:13 TLB

And let us not get tired of doing what is right, for after a while we will reap a harvest of blessing if we don't get discouraged and give up.　　　Galatians 6:9 TLB

The wicked flee when no man pursueth: but the righteous are bold as a lion.

Proverbs 28:1

FAILING ISN'T THE WORST THING IN THE WORLD — QUITTING IS.

We must be willing to accept responsibility for failure before we are able to accept responsibility for success. By accepting responsibility for failure, we open ourselves to be tested a second time and pass. Passing the test purifies us from the previous failure and replaces it with success.

Maturity does not come with age but begins with the acceptance of responsibility. Responsibility for success is built upon being responsible for failure. The person who is afraid to fail is generally the one who cannot handle success. God's pattern of success is to purify us of failures, give us fresh revelation from his Word, and lead us in "paths of righteousness" that end in success.

He restores my soul; He leads me in the paths of righteousness for His name's sake. Psalm 23:3 NKJV

A MAN IS QUALIFIED TO BE RESPONSIBLE FOR SUCCESS TO THE DEGREE HE IS WILLING TO BE RESPONSIBLE FOR FAILURE.

Faith and fear have the same definition. Faith is believing what you cannot see will come to pass. Fear is believing what you cannot see will come to pass.

Faith attracts the positive. Fear attracts the negative. The fear of failure is based on the fear of death. Humans are conditioned to failure. The earth shakes, grass dies, stars fall, businesses collapse, the body decays. Death is a constant, as is failure.

Give God the failures. Don't dwell on failure. The sum total of our lives can be measured by whether we operated on fear or faith. Dwelling on God's Word to build faith is where your strength and God's favor comes from.

So then faith comes by hearing, and hearing by the word of God.

Romans 10:17 NKJV

For God has not given us a spirit of fear, but of power and of love and of a sound mind.   2 Timothy 1:7 NKJV

FEAR ATTRACTS ATTACK.

Sin is a negative, and righteousness is a positive. That's why God requires us to confess *out* sin and also to confess *in* righteousness.

God inhabits the praises of his people. God does not inhabit gripes, complaints, or criticisms. In your communication with God, spill out every negative thing, then get to the point of praising him in spite of it all. Praise him out of obedience, and your emotions will eventually catch up. As you give God praises that he can inhabit, God will use your words to recreate your life. God's plan for you began with a positive and will always end with a positive.

If we confess our sins, He is faithful and just to forgive us our sins and to cleanse us from all unrighteousness.   1 John 1:9 NKJV

For with the heart one believes unto righteousness, and with the mouth confession is made unto salvation.   Romans 10:10 NKJV

But thou art holy, O thou that inhabitest the praises of Israel.   Psalm 22:3

But as for you, ye thought evil against me; but God meant it unto good. Genesis 50:20

GOD NEVER BUILDS ON THE NEGATIVE. HE ALWAYS BUILDS ON THE POSITIVE.

Carrying a grudge is holding something against someone —something God never does. Holding something against yourself for which you have asked God's forgiveness is a grudge God does not hold. God holds no grudges. When he forgets, he never remembers it against us anymore.

Christlike men learn to forgive as God forgives.

───────────────

Who will bring any charge against those whom God has chosen? It is God who justifies. Who then is the one who condemns? No one.   Romans 8:33-34 NIV

Receive the Holy Spirit. If you forgive the sins of any, they are forgiven them; if you retain the sins of any, they are retained.
                              John 20:22-24 NKJV

As far as the east is from the west, so far has he removed our transgressions from us.   Psalm 103:12 NIV

IF GOD FORGIVES US AND WE DO NOT FORGIVE OURSELVES, WE MAKE OURSELVES GREATER THAN GOD.

Tomorrow has never seen a failure. Any failure that comes today will soon be yesterday, and yesterday's dung is tomorrow's fertilizer.

Crises, setbacks, and occasional failures occur for everyone, but they cannot in and of themselves hurt you. Problems drive out the worst in you and bring out the best in you. The difference between people who fail and those who succeed often lies in how they handle the pressure of failure and adversity.

In front of every promise there is a problem. Don't look only at the problem, or you will lose sight of the promise.

I am come that they might have life, and that they might have it more abundantly.
John 10:10

Consider Him who endured such hostility from sinners, so that you will not grow weary and lose heart. Hebrews 12:3 NIV

YESTERDAY'S DUNG IS TOMORROW'S FERTILIZER.

Success is the greatest antidote to failure. If you want to complain about your failure and find others on whom to blame it, you'll live with that failure for life. If you want to get over failing, be successful.

Many men refuse to try for a better job, apply for the promotion, or launch a new business. They don't want to accept the responsibility for having their attempts fail. Success swallows failure.

Champions practice in private to succeed in public. Stay in until you win.

Watch ye, stand fast in the faith, quit [act] you like men, be strong.

1 Corinthians 16:13

I have fought the good fight, I have finished the race, I have kept the faith.

2 Timothy 4:7 NIV

CHAMPIONS ARE NOT THOSE WHO NEVER FAIL, BUT THOSE WHO NEVER QUIT.

On the darkest day, above the clouds, the sun is still shining. You may not see it with your eyes, but you know it is there. Circumstances, adversity, and hard times come and go, but above it all, God always has sunshine for your life.

Work can be hard or tedious, but it brings prosperity. You can always tell the manager or owner by the way they pick up, put away, straighten, or rearrange what is visible to the public. They see what the average worker fails to see. Do the work of the boss and one day you'll be the boss.

Regardless of what comes your way, remember to keep going. The clouds will soon be gone.

And we know that all things work together for good to them that love God, to them who are the called according to his purpose.　　Romans 8:28

Whatever you do, work at it with all your heart, as working for the Lord, not for human masters.　　Colossians 3:23 NIV

ABOVE THE CLOUDS, THE SUN ALWAYS SHINES.

UPWARD LEVELS

God orders our steps to take us from one level to the next, but at each stage, we start at the bottom again.

New levels require us to increase responsibility, knowledge, or authority. They call for further deepening of our character. Often, new levels require more of us than we want to give. Yet the more given, the more obtained. Levels can be vertical or horizontal. An army marches horizontally, but its ranks have levels of responsibility.

Passing through the stages of life that take us to new levels is a lifelong pattern that is inescapable for those who pursue success. The only way to avoid starting at the bottom of a new level is to avoid success.

The steps of good men are directed by the Lord. He delights in each step they take.
Psalm 37:23 TLB

Your word is a lamp for my feet, a light on my path. Psalm 119:105 NIV

Be renewed in the spirit of your mind.
Ephesians 4:23 NKJV

LIFE IS LIVED ON LEVELS THAT ARE ARRIVED AT IN STAGES.

Throughout life, we leave so we can enter. We leave the womb and enter infancy, leave infancy to enter childhood, leave childhood to enter adolescence, and on and on. Both leaving and entering create the crisis of change. The way you leave one stage is the way you will enter the next.

If your leaving was negative, always go with forgiveness for all. Don't bring negative seeds of the past into new fields. Put those experiences behind you by forgiving all. If your leaving was positive, never rest on faded glory. Let people judge you based on who you are, not what you were. Remember, when you experience success in one stage and start a new one, you start again at the bottom.

But one thing I do: forgetting what lies behind and reaching forward to what lies ahead, I press on toward the goal for the prize of the upward call of God in Christ Jesus.   Philippians 3:13-14 NASB

Do not call to mind the former things or consider things of the past.

                Isaiah 43:18 NASB

THERE ARE REALLY ONLY TWO THINGS YOU DO IN LIFE: ENTER AND LEAVE.

The better your business, the higher the level of life you'll achieve. Circumstances do not determine your level of life. What you do with circumstances determines your level in living.

The culture that provides the greatest opportunity for success lifts its entire civilization. The world's greatest handbook for learning economic basics is not found in the schoolbooks but in the Scriptures. Its truths create the highest level of society known on earth.

He who began a good work in you will carry it on to completion until the day of Christ Jesus.   Philippians 1:6 NIV

Trust in the LORD with all your heart and lean not on your own understanding; in all your ways submit to him, and he will make your paths straight.
                              Proverbs 3:5-6 NIV

BUSINESS IS NOT ABOUT MONEY OR TOYS, BUT THE LEVEL OF LIFE YOU WANT TO LIVE ON.

Water always seeks its own level. In terms of human life, this means you will always rise to the level of your faith.

If you believe you can make thousands per month, and move into a business that produces only hundreds, you will find a way to grow that business into thousands. If you have faith for hundreds per month and move into a business that produces thousands thinking you've hit the jackpot, the business will soon level out at hundreds per month.

What compels your mind, the hidden vision of your heart, the exercising of your faith will result in the way you live and the level you achieve.

For with God nothing shall be impossible.   Luke 1:37

For I say, through the grace given to me, to everyone who is among you, not to think of himself more highly than he ought to think, but to think soberly, as God has dealt to each one a measure of faith.   Romans 12:3 NKJV

EVERY MAN LIVES TO THE LEVEL OF HIS FAITH.

We sow to the future so we can reap from the past. Doing what is necessary when you don't feel like it is being instant in season and out of season and assures a meal at any time. The best salesman works during the storm when others are sitting by the fire.

Henry Ford built cars before there were roads on which to drive them. He influenced decision-makers to speed up the timing for the roads or he wouldn't have had a marketable product.

Life management begins with time management. Recognize your seasons of sowing.

He changes times and seasons; he deposes kings and raises up others. He gives wisdom to the wise and knowledge to the discerning.   Daniel 2:21 NIV

The sluggard will not plow by reason of the cold; therefore shall he beg in harvest, and have nothing.   Proverbs 20:4

He who gathers crops in summer is a prudent son, but he who sleeps during harvest is a disgraceful son.   Proverbs 10:5 NIV

EVERYTHING IN LIFE
IS SEASONAL. WE
CAN'T CHANGE THE
SEASONS. WE CAN
ONLY ADAPT TO THEM.

Men create the atmosphere of their lives by their attitude and words. Create an atmosphere of expectancy to prepare for success. Unemployed men with a loser attitude create a stifling atmosphere. Athletes with a winning attitude can charge a locker room or a whole stadium with the atmosphere of a winner. Fathers provide the atmosphere in the home, whether present or absent.

Charge your atmosphere with the expectation that God will act and unleash fresh creativity and productivity. These four words, while meditating on God's Word, can change the atmosphere of your life: "Expect God To Act."

But, O my soul, don't be discouraged. Don't be upset. Expect God to act!…He is my help! He is my God!

Psalm 42:11 TLB

Wait for the Lord; be strong and take heart and wait for the Lord.

Psalm 27:14 NIV

I wait expectantly, trusting God to help, for he has promised.   Psalm 130:5 TLB

EXPECTANCY IS THE ATMOSPHERE FOR MIRACLES.

INCREASE AND WEALTH

Obtaining a position on a baseball team is easier than maintaining it. Obtaining access to the boardroom of a publicly held company is easier than maintaining it. Obtaining riches is easier than maintaining a strong cash flow. Obtaining health is easier than maintaining healthy habits. And getting married is infinitely easier than maintaining a vibrant marriage for the next fifty years.

Anyone can make money. Managing and increasing is harder.

Many reasons exist for the difficulty in maintaining, but remember this important principle: It is possible for your talent to take you to a place your character cannot sustain. For that reason, we build character before we build our careers and our future.

And these are they likewise which are sown on stony ground; who, when they have heard the word, immediately receive it with gladness; And have no root in themselves, and so endure but for a time.

Mark 4:16-17

IT IS HARDER
TO MAINTAIN THAN
TO OBTAIN.

"Too many people buy things they don't need with money they don't have to impress people they don't like." I don't know who said that first, but it's good.

Jesus gave us this principle. Your heart follows your money. Where a man puts his money shows what he loves in life. If you want to see where your heart is, open your checkbook. The use of your money reveals more about your character than anything else.

For where your treasure is, there will your heart be also.   Matthew 6:21

A MAN'S AFFECTION FOLLOWS HIS MONEY.

Money represents your life. In return for giving your life at work, you receive money. The money you receive represents your time, talent, education, and experience. That means, how you spend your money shows what you do with your life.

Life's values are shown in the use of money. What you value most in life is where you invest most of your money, whether a car, sports, stock market, a wife, or the church.

If you want your life to count, make your money count. Master the principles that master money.

―――――――――――

No one can serve two masters. Either you will hate the one and love the other, or you will be devoted to the one and despise the other. You cannot serve both God and money.   Matthew 6:24 NIV

Then he said to them, "Watch out! Be on your guard against all kinds of greed; a man's life does not consist in the abundance of his possessions." Luke 12:15 NIV

WHAT YOU DO WITH YOUR MONEY SHOWS WHAT YOU DO WITH YOUR LIFE.

We are not the owners of anything; we are only stewards of everything we possess. We are stewards of talents, time, jobs, finances, children, ministries, and more. We possess a mind but don't own it. We are only a steward of it. Good stewardship maintains its capabilities.

We may possess a marriage, but we don't own a wife. We are only stewards of her love. Good stewardship maintains the marriage. Being a founder and owner of a company can be deceptive. Though owning the company, you are still only a steward.

Every man must give an account to God of his stewardship for all God has given him.

Moreover it is required in stewards, that a man be found faithful.   1 Corinthians 4:2

Command those who are rich in this present world not to be arrogant nor to put their hope in wealth…but to put their hope in God…. Command them to…be rich in good deeds, and to be generous and willing to share. In this way they will lay up treasure for themselves as a firm foundation for the coming age, so that they may take hold of the life that is truly life.   1 Timothy 6:17-19 NIV

MEN ARE STEWARDS, NOT OWNERS, OF WHAT THEY POSSESS.

Love is the desire to benefit others even at the expense of self because love desires to give. Lust is the desire to benefit self even at the expense of others because lust desires to get. Love is easily satisfied. Lust is insatiable. Love is the nature of heaven. Lust is the nature of hell.

Lust is seen on every level. Corporations can lust. Producing a short-term gain by sacrificing workers' raises can be motivated by lust. Employees can lust their jobs and cheat on hours or steal supplies. That's lusting the company's money, not doing a job to benefit the company.

To exhibit love is to work for someone else's highest good.

For the love of money is a root of all kinds of evils.   1 Timothy 6:10 ESV

When lust has conceived, it gives birth to sin; and when sin is full-grown, gives birth to death.   James 1:15 NIV

For all that is in the world, the lust of the flesh, and the lust of the eyes, and the pride of life, is not from the Father, but is of the world.   1 John 2:16

BOTH MONEY AND SEX ARE FOR LOVING AND GIVING, NOT LUSTING AND GETTING.

Prospering doesn't come down to how much you save, but how much you invest. This is true of money, love, faith, your body, and every virtue. The old axiom is, "Use it or lose it."

Divine math began with a command to Adam to multiply. Math for the purpose of growth and increase is not addition but multiplication. You add by saving, but you multiply by investing. Investing is simply putting money to its best use.

Any investment you make is always an investment of self. Investing time, talent, or money is investing self. Where you invest your money shows where your life is invested. In all your investment, invest in God's kingdom first. The more you give of yourself to God, the more you have to give.

The plans of the diligent lead to profit.
Proverbs 21:5 NIV

The wise store up choice food and olive oil, but fools gulp theirs down.   Proverbs 21:20 NIV

Give, and it will be given to you. Good measure, pressed down, shaken together, running over, will be poured into your lap.
Luke 6:38 NIV

THE LAW OF INCREASE AND DECLINE IS — BY USE YOU POSSESS AND INCREASE, BY DISUSE YOU DECLINE AND LOSE.

THE ULTIMATE: SERVING

Every work we do is service. Washing dishes, mowing the lawn, programming, milking the cow, selling a car—all are based on service.

Serving produces greatness. Amazon became one of the world's largest companies because of the number of people it served. The Source of all wisdom said, "He that would be greatest among you, let him be the servant of all" (Matthew 23:11). Companies become great based on how many people they serve. The better their product and the finer their service, the more they serve. The more they serve, the greater they become.

Let each of you look out not only for his own interests, but also for the interests of others.   Philippians 2:4 NKJV

Whosoever will be great among you, let him be your minister; And whosoever will be chief among you, let him be your servant: Even as the Son of man came not to be ministered unto, but to minister.
                              Matthew 20:26-28

THE MORE WE SERVE, THE GREATER WE BECOME.

Leaders can never stop serving, for when they do, they will no longer be qualified to lead. Serving is ministry. Learning to minister, serve capably and well, and work for the benefit of others are qualities that make a leader. Christ took a towel and washed his disciples' feet. Knowing when to be led and when to lead is the wisdom of a real leader.

Serving is not servitude. Serving is voluntary. Servitude is involuntary. A servant's heart is better than a ruler's mentality.

For even the Son of Man did not come to be served, but to serve, and to give his life as a ransom for many.   Mark 10:45 NIV

The greatest among you should be like the youngest, and the one who rules like the one who serves.   Luke 22:26 NIV

LEADERS ARE QUALIFIED TO LEAD TO THE DEGREE THEY ARE WILLING TO SERVE.

Christ proved his greatness in the sacrifice of himself for the sins of the world. Men prove it in their willingness to sacrifice themselves for the welfare of their family, employees, or fellow man. Some men are famous. Others are great.

———————————

Whoever welcomes this little child in my name welcomes me; and whoever welcomes me welcomes the one who sent me. For it is the one who is least among you all who is the greatest.   Luke 9:48 NIV

Your care for others is the measure of your greatness.   Luke 9:48 TLB

YOUR CARE FOR OTHERS IS THE MEASURE OF YOUR GREATNESS.

MAJORING IN MEN®
CURRICULUM

MANHOOD GROWTH PLAN

Order the corresponding workbook for each book, and study the first four Majoring in Men® Curriculum books in this order:

MAXIMIZED MANHOOD: Realize your need for God in every area of your life and start mending relationships with Christ and your family.

COURAGE: Make peace with your past, learn the power of forgiveness and the value of character. Let yourself be challenged to speak up for Christ to other men.

COMMUNICATION, SEX AND MONEY: Increase your ability to communicate, place the right values on sex and money in relationships, and greatly improve relationships, whether married or single.

STRONG MEN IN TOUGH TIMES: Reframe trials, battles and discouragement in light of Scripture and gain solid footing for business, career, and relational choices in the future.

Choose five of the following books to study next. When you have completed nine books, if you are not in men's group, you can find a Majoring in Men® group near you and become "commissioned" to minister to other men.

DARING: Overcome fear to live a life of daring ambition for Godly pursuits.

SEXUAL INTEGRITY: Recognize the sacredness of the sexual union, overcome mistakes and blunders and commit to righteousness in your sexuality.

THE UNIQUE WOMAN: Discover what makes a woman tick, from adolescence through maturity, to be able to minister to a spouse's uniqueness at any age.

NEVER QUIT: Take the ten steps for entering or leaving any situation, job, relationship or crisis in life.

REAL MAN: Discover the deepest meaning of Christlikeness and learn to exercise good character in times of stress, success or failure.

POWER OF POTENTIAL: Start making solid business and career choices based on Biblical principles while building core character that affects your entire life.

ABSOLUTE ANSWERS: Adopt practical habits and pursue Biblical solutions to overcome "prodigal problems" and secret sins that hinder both success and satisfaction with life.

TREASURE: Practice Biblical solutions and principles on the job to find treasures such as the satisfaction of exercising integrity and a job well done.

IRRESISTIBLE HUSBAND: Avoid common mistakes that sabotage a relationship and learn simple solutions and good habits to build a marriage that will consistently increase in intensity for decades.

JUST A BARTENDER: A captivating story of endurance and victory against overwhelming obstacles. The discovery of a man's identity against the backdrop of slavery, negative forces, and a world in turmoil. Stories that every man will identify with—to discover a new source of strength for himself.

ABOUT THE AUTHOR

Dr. Edwin Louis Cole (1922–2002), known as "the father of the Christian men's movement," was called by God to speak with a prophetic voice to the men of this generation. To that end, he founded the Christian Men's Network, a ministry that majors in men and communicates the reality that manhood and Christlikeness are synonymous.

A former pastor, evangelist, missionary, business executive, and denominational leader, Dr. Cole and his wife, Nancy, served the Lord together for more than fifty years. Over four million copies of his books are in circulation in more than forty languages, including his best-selling *Maximized Manhood*. Since his death, his legacy and vision have been carried on by his "sons" in the faith as they reach tens of thousands of men each month via books, videos, and other media.

Read more about the movement he started at CMN.men